# A Lil' Bit of This,

# A Lil' Bit of That

# &

# More

A catalog of the exhibition
"A Lil' Bit of This & A Lil' Bit of That"
Featuring the artwork of visual artist
Sálongo Lee
@
Black Heritage Gallery
Central School Arts & Humanities Center
Lake Charles, Louisiana
March 6-April 26, 2015

Sálongo's Art, LLC
P.O. Box 2011
Natchez, MS 39121-2011
www.salongosart.com
salongosart@gmail.com

Photography, Text & Design by Sálongo's Art, LLC
Library of Congress Cataloging-in-Publication Data
Lee III, J. R. Sálongo. 1947-

"A Lil' Bit of This, A Lil' Bit of That & More"
A catalog of the solo art exhibition of original photographs, mixed media constructions and Diddley Bows entitled "A Lil' Bit of This & A Lil' Bit of That" by the visual artist known as Sálongo Lee. It is also a collection of images of original artwork and haiku poetry that was not included in the gallery exhibition.
By J. R. Sálongo Lee III ©2015

# Art, Photography and Poetry Books By The Artist

Haiku Dreams: Voices From My Third Eye Vol. II
Coming November 30, 2015

Black & White Reflections:
Original Haiku and Photography
2014

Southern Road Trips Mississippi & Louisiana Vol. 1
2011

Haiku Dreams: Voices From My Third Eye Vol. 1
2010

# Collaboration On Design & Layout

Moments In Time, The Art of
Charles R. Crossley, Sr. Book #1: 2000-2012
2013

All My Books Are Available On www.Amazon.com

## The Introduction:

Celebrating the Arts in Southwest Louisiana since 2001, the Black Heritage Gallery is excited to welcome photographer, visual artist and self-published author Sálongo Lee for a much anticipated second solo exhibition and book signing. "From There, To Here, To There" in 2009 was his first exhibition in the gallery. His exhibition of photography and handmade books was very well received. As a guest curator for the gallery in 2011 Sálongo organized a group exhibition entitled "Conversations South By South West". He gathered a group of seven painters and photographers from California, Louisiana and Mississippi to exhibit their artwork along with his photography.

I'm excited that Sálongo wanted to have his upcoming solo exhibition, "A Lil' Bit of This & A Lil' Bit of That" in our gallery. This is his first solo exhibition in six years, which includes recent photographs, mixed media constructions and handcrafted Diddley Bows (a one string guitar). The gallery will also host the signing of his fourth book of photography, mixed media constructions and original haiku poetry. Entitled "A Lil' Bit of This, A Lil' Bit of That & More" is not only a catalog of the artwork in the exhibition. The (& More) in the title refers to images of artwork in progress and excepts of haiku poetry for "Haiku Dreams: Voices From My Third Eye Vol. II" that is due out November 30, 2015.

Sálongo is a California artist who has been on an extended sojourn or Walk-About to the South. Since 2007 he has lived in Natchez, Mississippi, a small town on the bluffs overlooking the river. He is a recipient of multiple artist grants, honorariums and a Fellowship In Photography from the Mississippi Arts Commission. He is also a member of the Mississippi Arts Commission's Artist Roster and is one of their Arts Ambassadors; Sálongo is also active in the Louisiana art scene. As a member of the New Orleans Photo Alliance he has exhibited in their gallery and in One Night, One Hundred Photographers held at the New Orleans Museum of Modern Art. Sálongo is also a member of The Greater Baton Rouge Arts Council.

This exhibition of art by Sálongo Lee fits our mission of being a catalyst for the creative expression of artists and the active engagement of the community in supporting the arts. By presenting outstanding and committed artists from across the country and from within the region to our community our local artists are inspired. Our community will understand the importance of supporting the artists and art organizations that contribute to making our community a wonderful place to live.

Stella Miller, Black Heritage Gallery Curator

**Black Heritage Gallery:**

A gallery that exhibits works by local and regional artists to showcase the achievements and impact of the African American community in Southwest Louisiana. The gallery is located in the Central School Arts & Humanities Center, which was originally an elementary school. The Center is located at 809 Kirby Street, Suite 207 in Lake Charles. Black Heritage Gallery opened June 28, 2001 with a grant from the Junior League of Lake Charles, Inc.

The opening exhibition honored the baseball legends of the Negro National Leagues and the hometown heroes of Southwest Louisiana. Located in the historic Central School, it is among the 26 initial sites on Louisiana's African-American Heritage Trail that was announced in February 2008.

## Artist Statement:

Photography has been my primary medium of creative expression for over 50 years. As I traveled this path as an artist, how I create art has been affected by my life experiences and the changes in the tools and technology used in the creation and viewing of art. I have embraced these changes and have learned to use a variety tools and mediums of creative expression to bring my visions and imagination into existence for the world to experience.

Sálongo Lee
Natchez, Mississippi Studio February 20, 2015

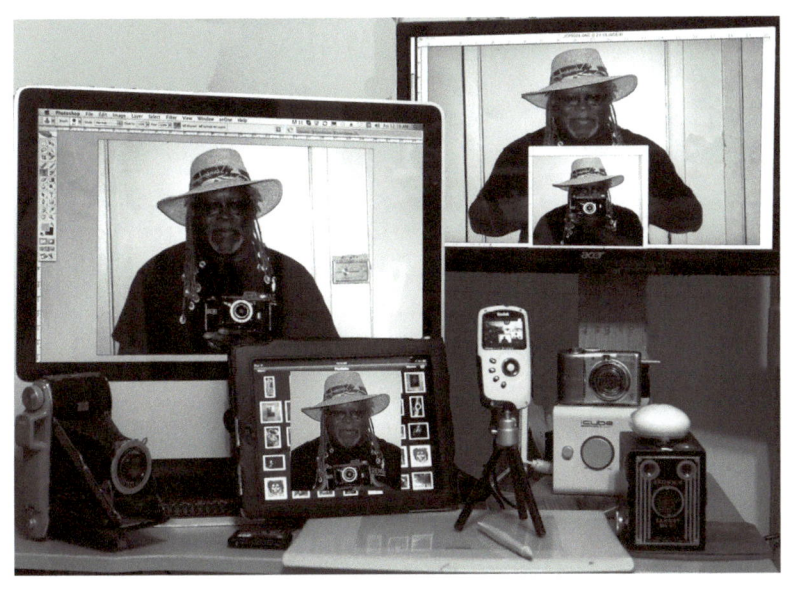

The Artist In The Natchez Cave

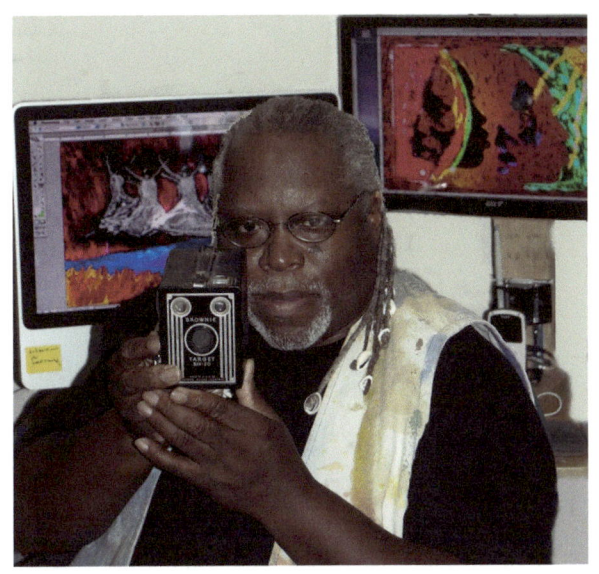

# The Catalog

## The Exhibition:

It has been six years since my last solo exhibition in a gallery other than ArtsNatchez Gallery, the artist run gallery I have belonged to since 2008. I have been on an artist sojourn or Walk-About these past eight years since I moved to Mississippi in 2007.

My primary medium of artistic expression is photography. But this gift of time has allowed me to explore other means of creative expression such as Impasto or Palette Knife painting, sculpture with polymer and air dried clays, mixed media collage and monoprinting and self publishing books of my haiku poetry and artwork.

I'm having this exhibition to share some of the imagery and poetry I have created during this time and to give a peek at some of my artwork and projects in progress or are nearing completion. I hope to do more solo and group exhibitions over the next 18 months before my wife (who is my best friend, 1st assistant and muse) and I return to California, which is home.

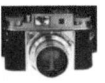

## The Photography:

I have been learning and exploring photography for over fifty years beginning in sixth grade in East Orange New Jersey. I started with an old Kodak Brownie camera photographing anything and everything that caught my eye. The idea that I could capture what I saw on a piece of celluloid film and with a few chemicals from the local drug store I could develop that film and with some special paper and chemicals I could then make contact prints was nothing short of magic.

I was given an enlarger and set up my first darkroom in the attic of my family home when I was twelve years old. I was hooked and I loved the magic of photography and have witnessed major changes. Now that magic has been enhanced with digital cameras, the computer, software and photo lab quality home printers. My home printer is a lot larger than the average personal printer. Besides being able to print photographs as large as 24"x40", I can also print on almost any material if I can get it into the printer. I cannot wait to get a printer that will allow me to print 40"x60" photographs and to print on glass.

I use photography to create more than just pretty pictures. I like to push the boundaries of what a photograph is. I want to construct images and print my visions and imagination from My Third Eye. I want to speak to the world with my images.

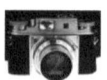

## Constructed Photographs:

I manipulate images in the computer and print directly onto wood, fabric or metal foil. The image may be further altered when it is mounted onto a support, such as a wood panel and various finishes can be applied. I want you to touch the image and feel texture.

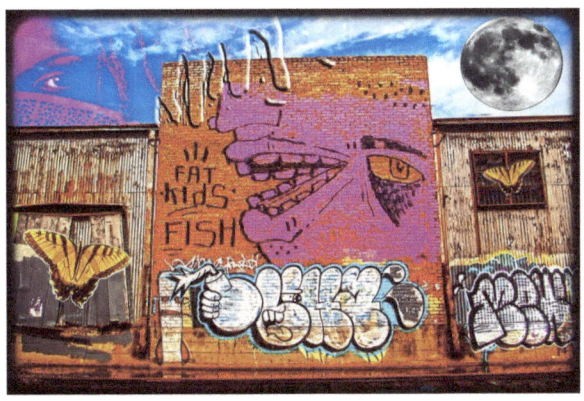

"Fat Kids Fish Under The Eye of The Moon Goddess"
New Orleans ©2015 Photo Mounted on Wood Panel

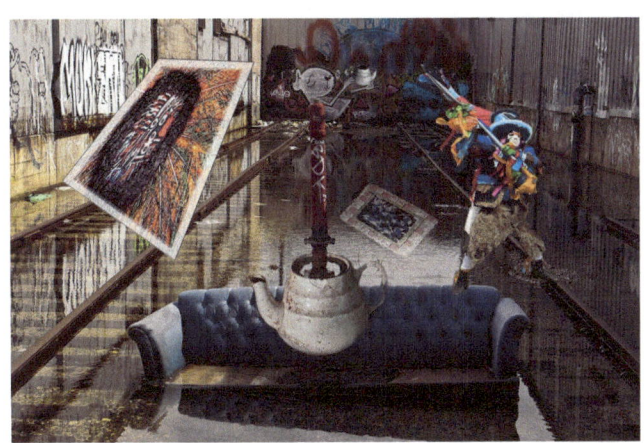

"Mad Mouse Tea Party In the Alley"
New Orleans ©2015 Photo Mounted on Wood Panel

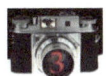

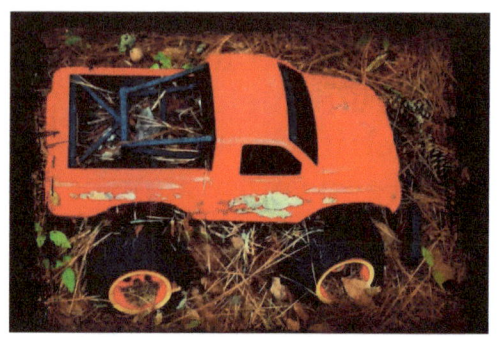

"Little Red Truck"  ©2015
Photo Mounted on Canvas Panel with Textured-
Borders Created with Acrylic Modeling Paste

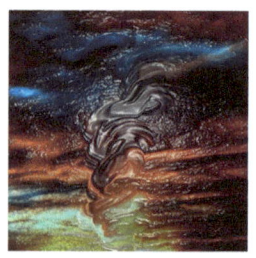
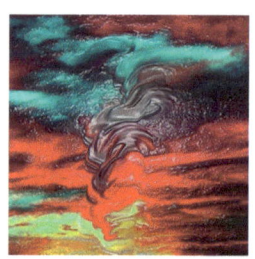
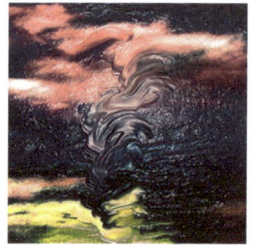

Whirlwind #1    Whirlwind #2    Whirlwind #3

Triptych #1  ©2015 Photo Printed on Gallery
Wrapped Canvas Stretcher Frames

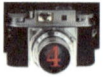

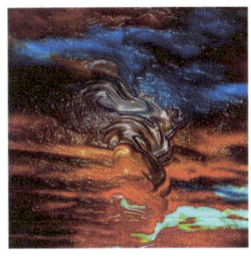 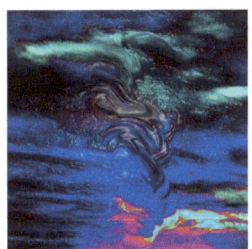 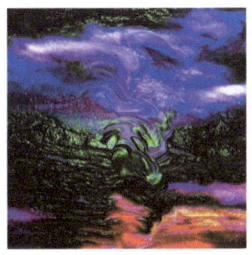

Whirlwind #4    Whirlwind #5    Whirlwind #6

Triptych #2 ©2015 Photo Printed on Gallery
Wrapped Canvas Stretcher Frames

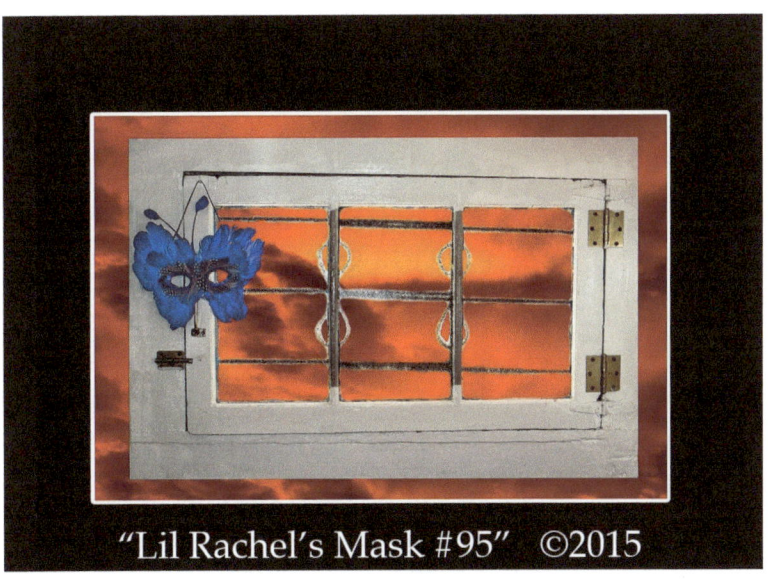

"Lil Rachel's Mask #95"  ©2015

Photo Mounted on Wood Panel with Textured
Border Created with Acrylic Modeling Paste

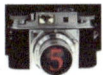

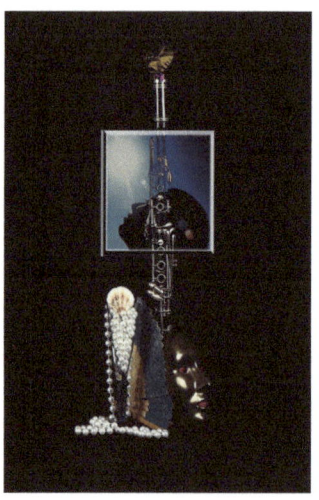

"Magic Butterfly Solo" ©2014
Still Life with 110 Year Old Trumpet, Bamboo Fan,
Beads, Wine Glass, Sea Shell and Brass Face Mask
Mounted on Wood Panel

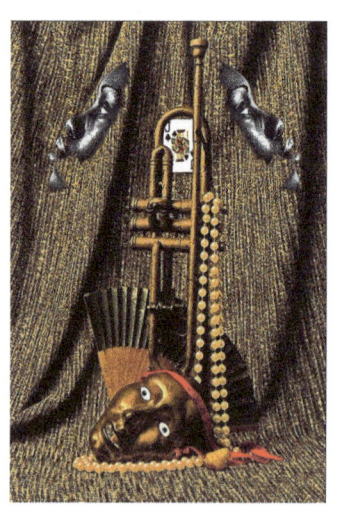

"I'll Put A Spell On You" ©2014
Still Life with 110 Year Old Trumpet, Bamboo
Fan, Beads, Playing Card, Painted Eyes Brass Face
Mask and Ribbon Mounted on Wood Panel

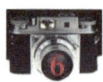

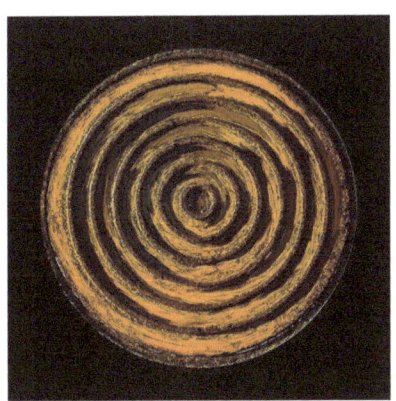

"Circles" ©2013
Photo of Man Hole Cover Printed on Watercolor
Paper Mounted on Circular Wood Panel

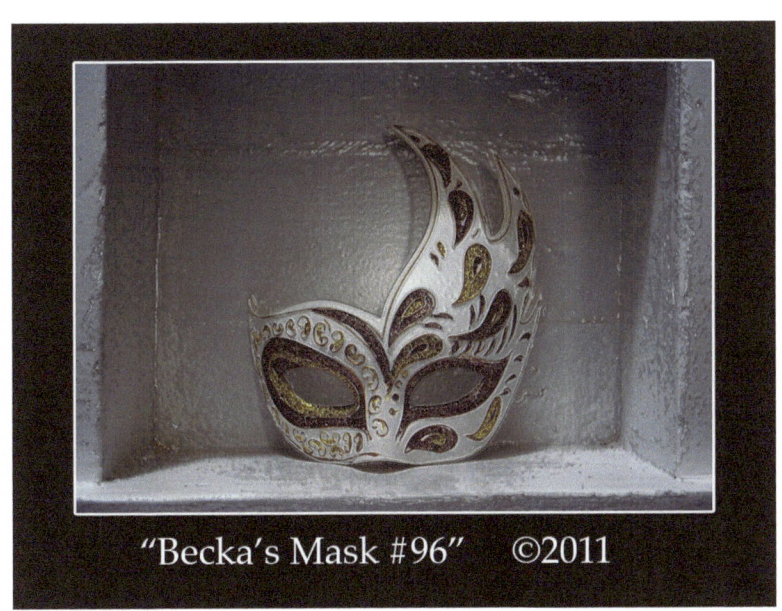

"Becka's Mask #96"    ©2011

Printed on Watercolor Paper

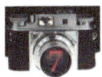

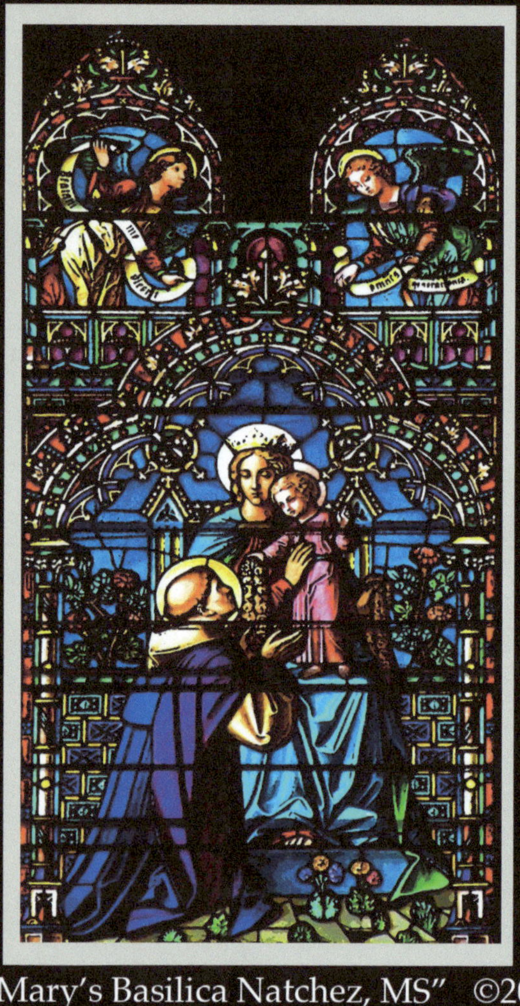

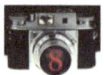

"St Mary's Basilica Natchez, MS" ©2011
Printed on Aluminum Foil

Mounted on Wood Panel with Textured Border
Created with Acrylic Modeling Paste

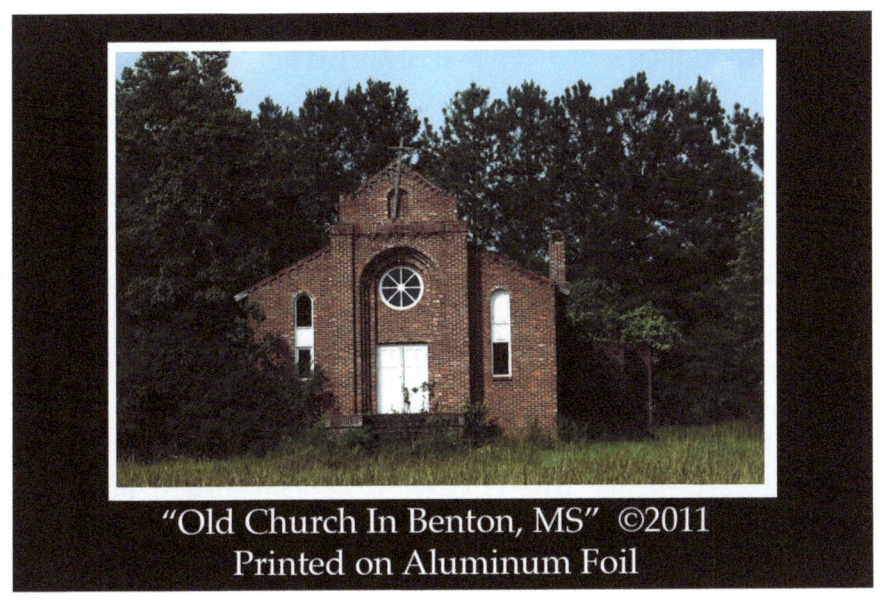

"Old Church In Benton, MS" ©2011
Printed on Aluminum Foil

Images, such as the one above must be seen to fully
appreciate the luminance and the texture that comes
from printing on alternative surfaces such as fabrics,
aluminum foil and even acrylic paint skins.

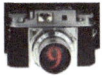

## Mixed Media Constructions:

I like working with my hands as there is more of a connection to the artwork when physically touching, shaping and texturing the materials used in the creation of the work. I am not a painter. I cannot draw, but I love using heavy bodied acrylic mediums, gels and different materials in my work.

I thank the late McComb, Mississippi artist, Charles R. Crossley, Sr. for exposing me to the joys of working with materials like glass beads, modeling paste sand and tools, such as Palette Knives to apply paint and other mediums to wood or canvas. I also sculpt elements using Polymer Clays and embed objects and photographs into the piece.

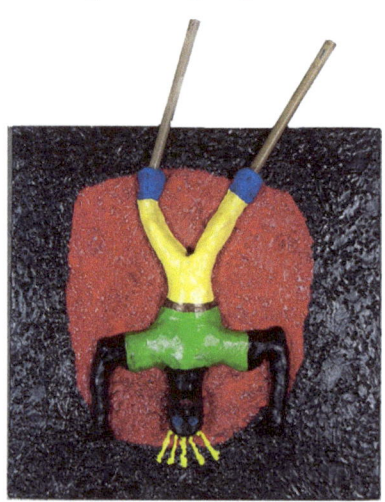

"Stilt Dancer #6" ©2015
Polymer Clay, Acrylic Paint, Modeling Paste,
Bamboo and Glass Beads on Wood Panel

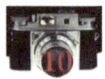

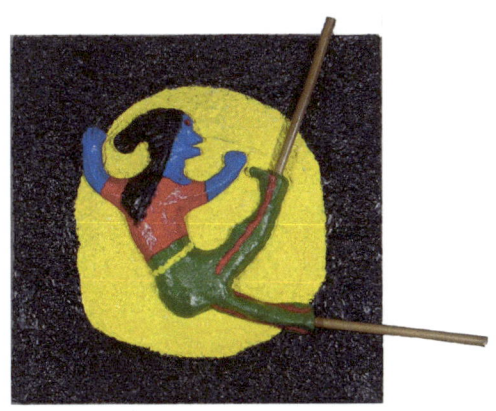

"Stilt Dancer #5"  ©2015
Polymer Clay, Acrylic Paint, Modeling Paste,
Bamboo and Glass Beads on Wood Panel

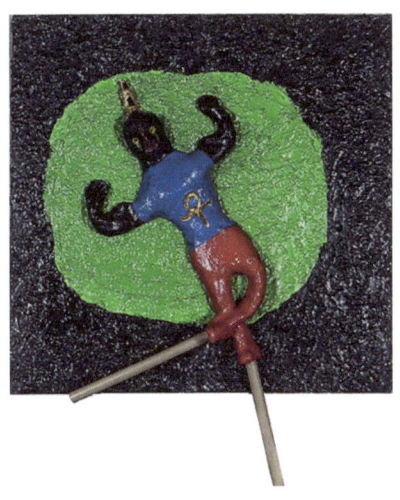

"Stilt Dancer #4"  ©2015
Polymer Clay, Acrylic Paint, Modeling Paste,
Bamboo and Glass Beads on Wood Panel

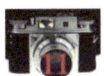

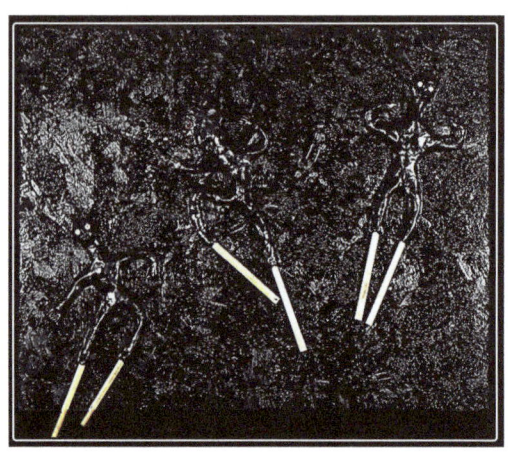

"Stilt Dancer #3" ©2014
Polymer Clay, Acrylic Paint, Modeling Paste,
Bamboo and Glass Beads on Wood Panel

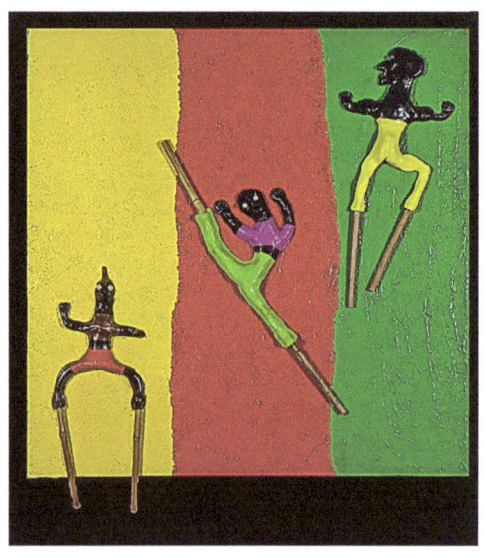

"Stilt Dancer #2" ©2014
Polymer Clay, Acrylic Paint, Modeling Paste,
Bamboo and Glass Beads on Wood Panel

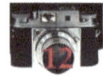

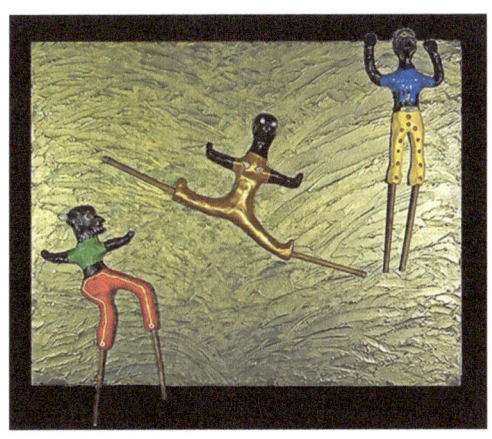

"Stilt Dancer #1" ©2014
Polymer Clay, Bamboo, Beads and
Acrylic Paint on Wood Panel

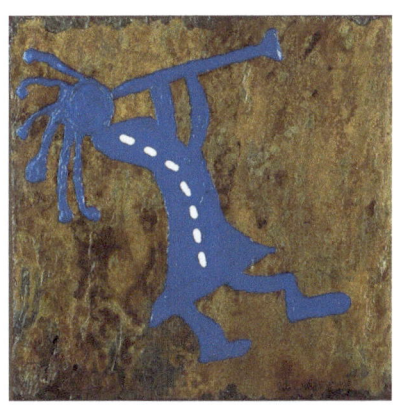

"Kokopelli #2" ©2011
Acrylic Dimensional Paint on Slate"

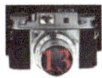

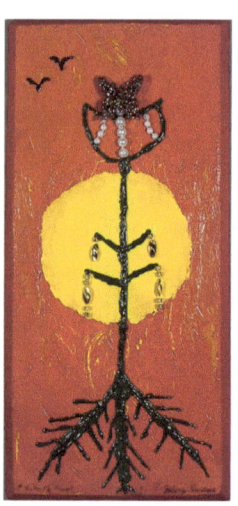

"Butterfly Flower" ©2012
Impasto Acrylic Painting, Mardi Gras Beads, Glitter and Plastic Butterfly on Wood Panel

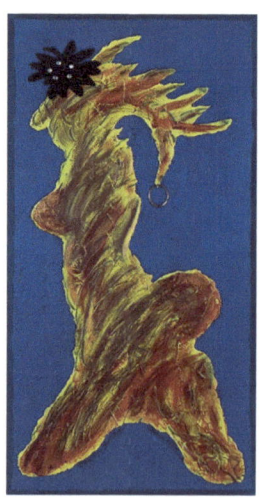

"Struttin' Her Stuff" ©2010
Impasto Acrylic Painting, Earring, Fabric with Costume Jewelry on Wood Panel

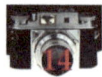

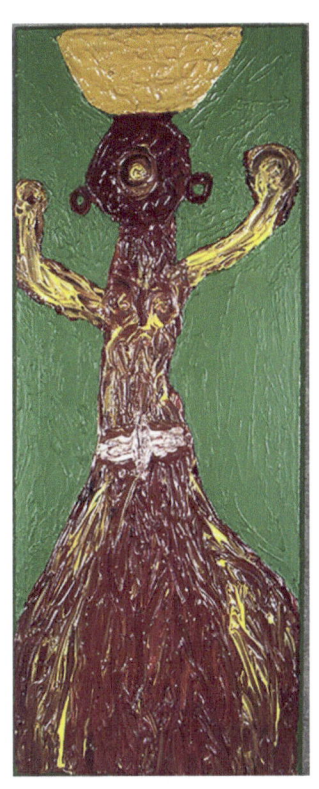

"Woman With Basket" ©2010
Impasto Acrylic Painting on Wood Panel

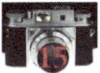

# Diddley Bows:

People ask: What are Diddley Bows and how did I come to make a musical instrument that I do not play as of yet? I learned about them when the late Mississippi artist, Charles R. Crossley, Sr. lent me the book "Circle Dance", which was about his friend and New Orleans artist John Scott. It was in the collection of images of his sculptures that I came across a piece entitled "Diddley Bow". It was a metal sculpture of a one string guitar, which piqued my curiosity about the origins of this instrument.

I learned that the instrument's origin is West African and was typically made as a children's toy by slaves in the American South. It was usually the first instrument that the early blues musicians learned to play until they could afford to buy a guitar. It was simple to make. All you needed was a board, some nails, a glass jar or tin can and broom wire. It is played by plucking the string and the tone is changed by sliding the broken neck of a glass bottle or a piece of metal along the string like a slide guitar.

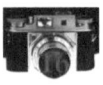

Though it was first documented in the rural South in the 1930's; numerous blues musicians played them, one even took his name from the instrument-Bow Diddley. Since it was considered a childs' instrument and toy; many musicians did not continue to play it as an adult. That being so, today there are some notable musicians like jazz pianist Cooper-Moore, American blues man Seasick Steve, Samm Bennett, Danny Kroha, One String Willie, and blind musician Velcro Lewis and Jack White who play the Diddley Bow in live performances and recording sessions.

I started making them as functional works of art in 2012. My Diddley Bows are one of kind and can be played. I use found objects, cabinet hardware and broom wire. The one material that I use that dates back to rural South and the early musicians is broom wire, which is becoming harder to find as modern brooms are being made more from synthetic materials instead of straw. These brooms do not require wire for their construction. I've been fortunate that blues musician One String Willie has been able to find a supply and I've ordered a few more coils so I can continue to make my unique Diddley Bows and eventually learn to play one.

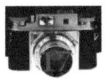

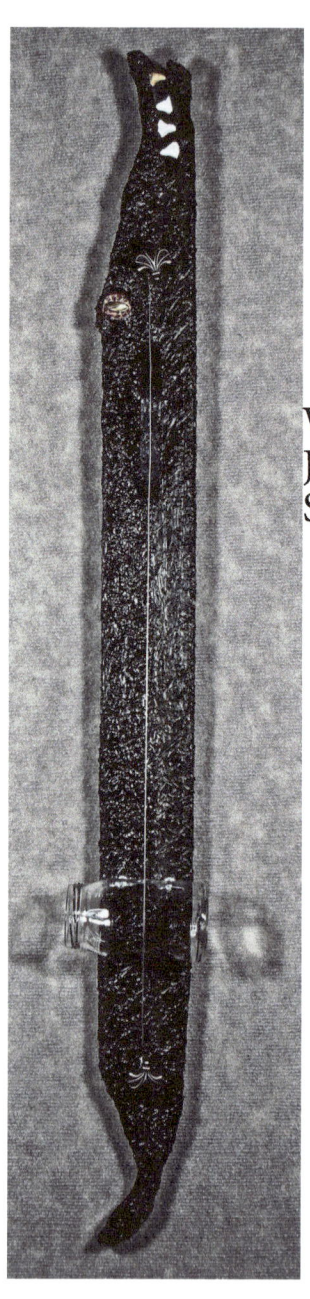

"Diddley Bow (Gator) #3"

©2015
Wood Board, Cabinet Hardware,
Jelly Jar, Acrylic Paint, Teeth
Sculpted from Polymer Clay and
Broom wire

"Diddley Bow (Hwy 61) #5"

©2012
Wood Board, Cabinet Hardware, Tequila Bottle, Aluminum Foil, Acrylic Paint, Steel Bolts and Broom wire

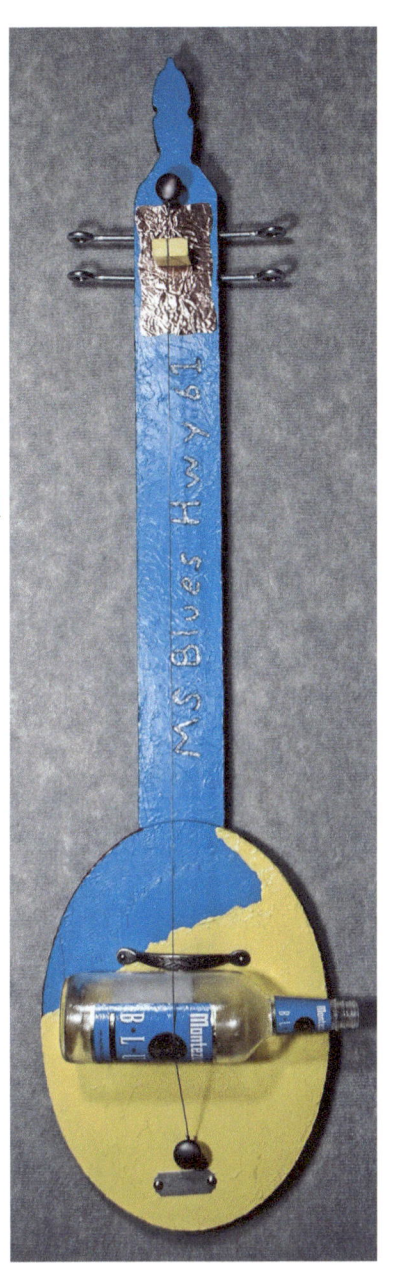

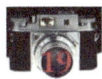

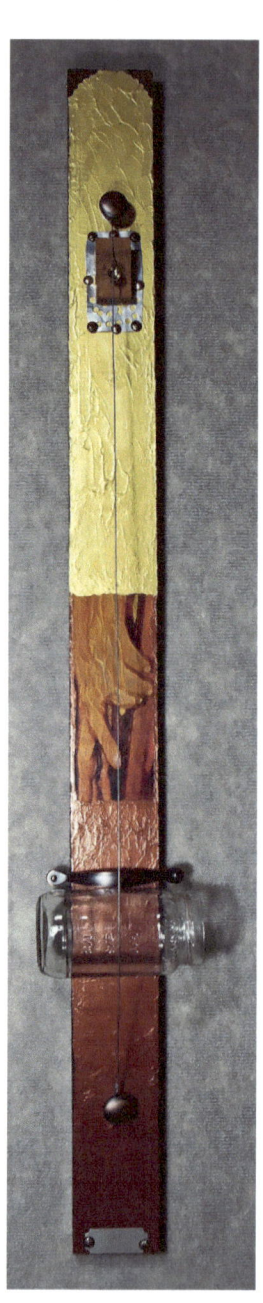

"Diddley Bow #3 (Finger Picker)"

©2012
Wood Board, Cabinet Hardware, Mason Jar, Metal Foil Acrylic Paint, metal foil, Broom wire and a Photo of New Orleans musician Theresa Anderson's fingers.

# & More

I want to share some works in progress that I will present in future art exhibitions and self-published books. To see more please visit my web site and sign up for my e-mail newsletter.
www.salongosart.com

**Haiku Dreams: Voices From My Third Eye Vol. II**
**Coming November 30, 2015**

The rest of my life
Started with eyes opening
And first breath of air

Friends are like seasons
They come when it is their time
And linger past their time

Time is so fleeting
It moves like the blowing wind
Stopping for nothing

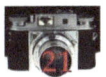

Love is an ocean
　　Restless and always moving
　　　　Flooding our open heart

If you have no dreams
　　Life is like running in place
　　　　You'll get nowhere fast

Run no walk no run
　　Do not panic this is life
　　　　Making Decisions

**Photography Works In Progress:**

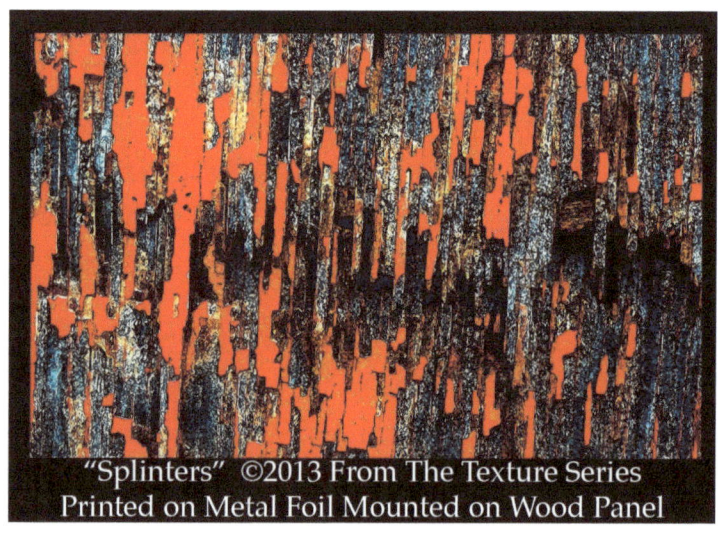

"Splinters" ©2013 From The Texture Series
Printed on Metal Foil Mounted on Wood Panel

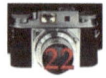

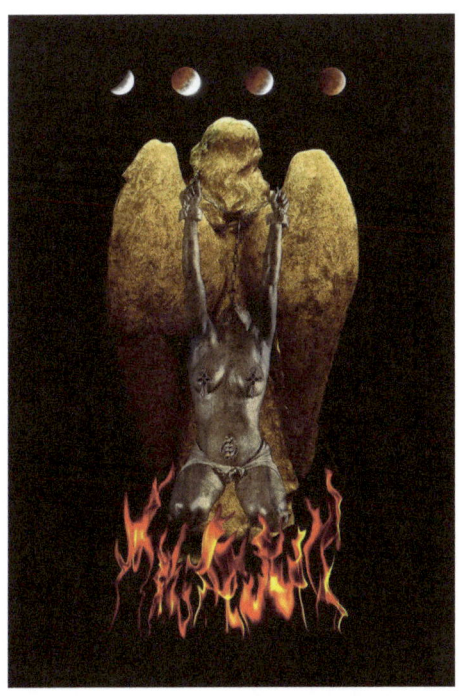

"Shelter Me Under Your Wings, Oh Lord" ©2015
From The Series Inspired By Music

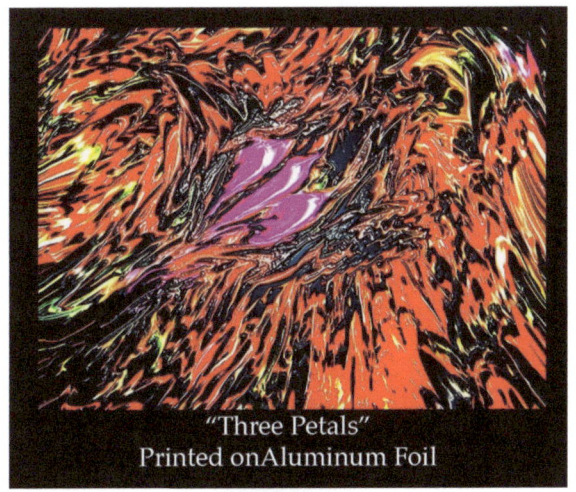

"Three Petals"
Printed onAluminum Foil

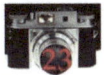

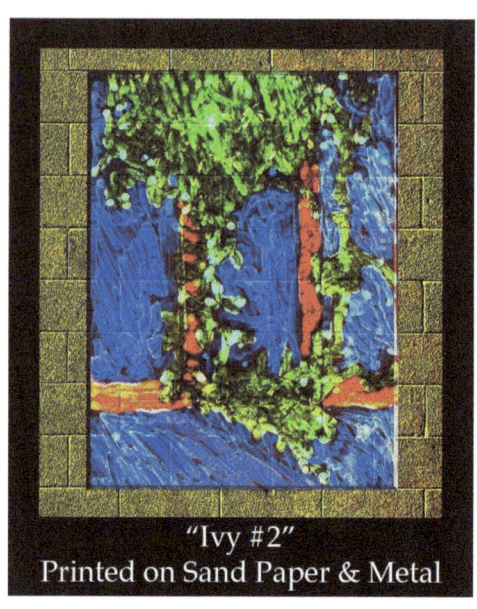

"Ivy #2"
Printed on Sand Paper & Metal

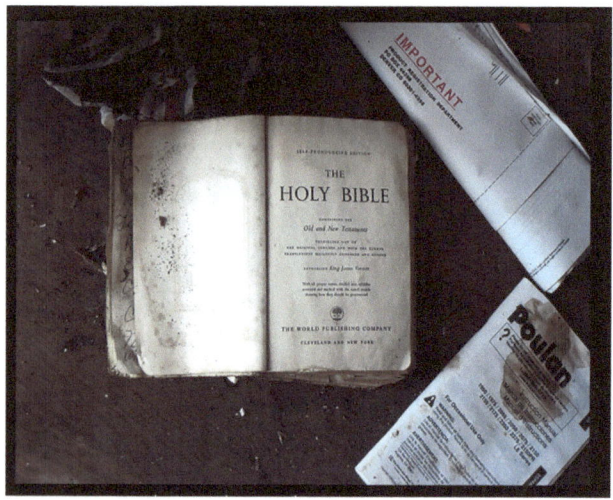

"Is It Not Needed Anymore?"
From The Abandoned Project: Part II
An Exhibition & Book Due 2016

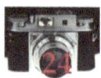

Once Again I Must Pay Tribute To
My wife, Best Friend, Muse and Editor.
Without Her Support and Understanding
This Project Would Not Have Been Possible.

She Made Sure I Had Food, Drink, Fresh Sheets On
The Bed And That I Would Come Out of The Cave At
Least Once A Day For Human Contact And A Hug.

Much Love, Kisses and Thanks To My

## Lady Daphne

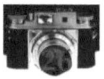